Read Me
Connecting the
Dots

I0477947

Alonzeonia R.
Ellison

DEDICATION

I dedicate this book to myself, my family, and my friends.
Most importantly, God.

CONTENTS

ACKNOWLEDGMENTS

To God whom I love, God is real.

1 CHAPTER

A thought of college crossed my mind, as I sat on my living room sofa. Me, Rose, now at the age of eighteen, with only six more months until my High School Graduation.

I had spent the past three years of high school, not giving my best. The site of paper-work made me sleepy, and I had just in that moment taken college into consideration.

And with a "C" average `` which University would accept me?

I should have known better than to even consider the idea of College.

But all of the other Seniors joyed with the conversation of College, which had left the idea of it very heavy on my mind, and "fun" one way to describe what the College experience would be like.

And let me be honest, College would be a great route to take, and a perfect way for me to make it out of my small town, Georgetown, GA.

Even though the thought of moving away from home for College put a little fear in me.

The thought of, which new City/State would be my new Home? Filled me with excitement.

Although the thought of, What would I go to study for, did not excite me, very much for I had no special skills.

I had so many questions on my mind.

Enough of stressing College, and my future plans, it was Friday night.

The night of Evan's, A friend of mine from High School, Birthday Party. It was time for me to get ready for a Great night.

Jane, and Amber, Girls who had been my two best-friends since our very first day of High school, ninth grade year, would pick me up from my house for the Party.

They say, "The biggest leap of faith you will take in your entire life will be the distance in between Middle school and High school, where you leave your old friends behind to find new ones".

When I met the two of them in Mrs. Wilkes "Cooking class", my life was complete in that moment.

And there was also Kate, my other best-friend, it was just the four of us, in a "Friendship", but in that Class is where we all became so very close.

Having the best conversations, many laughs and giggles.

Kate had been M.I.A lately. Who knew where she was? It had been Months now, since I had last seen her around School, that was not like her, things were becoming a tab bit off, and I was becoming worried, I hoped to hear from her soon, it had just been the four us, sticking together, throughout the past three years of our High School Journey, and things were going good, as so it seemed.

Then again I did not have much time to worry, for I knew Kate would come back around.

2 CHAPTER

I began getting ready for Evan's party, with my favorite Song "Beyonce x Nicki minaj x Feelin Myself" playing in the background had taken my mind completely off the idea of College.

With my outfit already laid out, and hair done, A long weave ponytail, down my back, "Nicki, inspired", I was truly feeling myself. I stood in the mirror, as I put on my tight fitted jeans and a white tank top, it did not take much for me to get "Cute". I was in my Heart the most beautiful girl in the world.

I stood, five foot, two inches, with dark brown gazing eyes, carrel skin, pretty plumed lips, and an hourglass figure.

Born back here to Earth as "Mona Lisa", the most beautiful picture ever painted, I believed.

"The easiest way to kill a girl, is to tell her that she is not the mirror image of Beauty, that She sees herself in her Own heart".

So no one could tell me any differently.

I had just put on my shoes, as the horn blew, "Beep, Beep, Beep, Beep!

"I am coming", I screamed as I ran out of my front door.

When we arrived at the party, all eyes were on us. Of course we were the most good looking girls in school, We also shined like Diamonds. Who were we to think we would be the only "Stars" in the party, when "Chris and his boys" walked into the place, all heads turned, They were just some cute boys from school, to me, I was not interested.

We all enjoyed the night, the party was amazing, great music and good people was all I needed at that moment.

As I got ready for bed, I smiled at what an amazing night we shared.

To bed I went.

3 CHAPTER

Ouch!

I woke up out of my sleep, screaming.

A sharp pain down the center of my spine, As I tried arising from my bed, the pain grew deeper, I was leaking blood, my spine was slowly cracking.

I was dying, as my voice weakened, my faith weaved less, my eyes rolled to the back of my head, there was death.

I felt it, I saw it, I knew it, "I watched it slowly happening, I was giving up, and Who had known "death" would be so Beautiful.

The sun was rising, the ocean was smooth sailing, the birds were singing to me, the wind was holding me so tight. I was laying out on a beach, I was dead. Death was on a beach, death made me say, "AH, I am here".

Death was peace, but peace was not ready for me, it seemed.

I reopened my bloody eyes, no room for tears, back up. I was laid out on a Hospital bed, screaming and kicking for answers, only answers, I needed to know what was killing me, I had no idea of what was going on, or what would happen next. Or why I did not, could not die?

"When we die, all we do next is rebirth". Who was I to think I would be able to escape to the Ocean that easily, by simply dying, and floating away.

With Doctors and Nurses surrounding me, put me in more of a panic.

I was wondering why death sent me back to life.

I looked deep into one of the nurses eyes as she held my head up, telling me "things would be okay!", a young white lady, blonde hair, light deep, blue eyes, struck me as I was put to sleep.

4 CHAPTER

Hello, Rose!

I am God, The guide, I am here, Open your eyes, Open your eyes, please, Rose open your eyes.

He laid hands on me, and my whole body popped back into place.

I opened my eyes, and I was standing.

Wow! Wow! Wow! My eyes were busted wide open.

There stood, God.

A tall white, glowing faced figure, dark gazing black eyes, nice long hair pulled back into a ponytail, a long faced bread, covered in a white robe, no shoes, barefoot, he was standing with the wind, holding him, he was, flowing.

As I stood there with a bloody, hospital gown on, face filled with fears.

Come with me, he asked, as he reached for my hand, I placed my hand in the palm of his hand.

Now, close your eyes, I am "The guide", all I ask is that you Trust me.

Do not open your eyes until I say so.

Open! He said.

I opened my eyes.

Do you know where we are he asked, as he guided me to a front door, that read,

"Welcome to Kate's, Slumber party".

Kate's house, yes, I answered.

Why are we here, I asked.

Well, he explained, There is something here that you buried years ago.
"Something I buried," I paced.
What do you mean? Something I buried, I asked.
-

After a moment of wondering, The night came back to me, so vividly..

I buried it.

A letter, I shouted.
A letter? He responded.
Yes, A letter, I said again.

Well you see, It was all Jane Idea, to bury Letters.

"Jane had watched an interview on" The Oprah Winfrey Show". There was a young black lady on the Show, explaining how she became a "Millionaire".
She had buried a letter, "A Birthing of a New Form of Life" Letter, an old tradition.

Her Letter stated that she would become a Millionaire, Business Woman/Owner, by the age of twenty-three.
Her business was to create an Empire, in designing Shoes, The hottest brand Shoe we all see, and wear today. She was only Seventeen at the time, and she was Rich by the age of twenty-three.

She buried her Letter, as if it was a seed and it grew as a flower, Sunflower, she explained.
She walked in the "LIGHT" of it you see? I asked.

"But, "The Letter" must start it, "I am, followed by your name, followed by "your sentence" and it MUST end with a (.) period at the end of your Letter.

5 CHAPTER

Do you remember what your Letter Stated, he asked.

Yes! I answered.

It was very short.

We all buried Letters that night, Me, Kate, Jane, and Amber. The four of us ripped out a page of paper from Kate's notebook.

"I am Rose, I will marry Justin, And we will have a daughter, June, Will be her name, She will be very gorgeous, she will have Red hair, with light brown eyes, she will be the light, and she will shine so bright!

We will live happily ever after."

"Justin", The star of the High School Basketball team, he was so fine! He stood at least six foot, he was light skinned and he had colorful eyes, it was as they changed from blue to grey every time I looked at him. Every time I looked at him he took my breath away, I would be walking down the hallways, and I would see him, through the passing way. I would almost get lost in his eyes, clumsy he made me, and very shy, not all the time did I speak, I would sometimes see him and just smile. I had the most amazing smile.

I never even told him I had the biggest crush on him, and it was as if he had "Rose's Husband" on his back, because that was all I saw when he would turn away.

Do you remember where you buried your letter? God asked.

Yes, I walked right over to it, right under the tree in front of Kate's front yard, where there was only one tree.

You may speak things into existence, you may draw them, write them, sing them, when you envision a thing it is here. Simply walk into it.

The whole entire journey here on "Earth" is to give birth, to create, to SEE, those things in Life form.

What a Blessing to know, He said again.

"YOU ALL, ALL OF MY CHILDREN, WERE BIRTHED HERE, ON EARTH, WITH A GIFT, A CANVAS, AT YOUR FOOT, WITH ALL OF THE TOOLS TO MATCH, FOR FREE, WITH A MESSAGE BEHIND IT OF COURSE, THE MESSAGE, "CREATE".

Simple you see? He questioned.

7 CHAPTER

She is not mine!

I looked at him, dead in the face and said.

I was not pregnant, I am still a Virgin.

I was just thinking of college and of what I would do with my life, and now I have a freaking baby, you're telling me.

This can not be true, I cried. Looking back at June, My heart, wanting so desperately to melt.

He grabbed my hand. Pulled me into, hospital, room door 3C, we burst in and there, lied Kate.

I screamed and ran to her, Kate! Kate! Are you okay? I asked, and asked.

She can not hear you, he explained, many different worlds you see? Many different Gods, many different, Me.

"I am here to Teach you", he said.

 He said.

Let me explain.

"The Letter".

As you know it, a very true tradition discovered many years ago, what a blessing to know.

You write into form what you want, Bury it. And it comes to form. A seed that grows into a flower. Simple. "You walk into that Light, and the Light grows".

 A creation of a new world, for self, a seed, to bury, Again as you walk in the light of it, the seed truly grows.

A Birthing of a New Life, or Life Path, I like to say, A journey for you to take. Bringing a "Thing" into existence.

There are many ways to bring things into existence, into form in this World, on Planet Earth.

I almost fell in love.

6 CHAPTER

I dug, and I dug, but the Letter I once buried was not there.

I looked back up to God, it is not here, I cried.

Come, come, he demanded.

I gave him my hand, once again.

His touch, so soft, so warm, so loving.

Close your eyes, he said, I did.

Open! He said.

I opened my eyes, we were back in the hospital, but now we were standing in the window, with my bloody hospital gown, where the New Born babies lay.

But there was only one baby.

This is June, he smiled.

June? I shouted! The baby from the Letter you mean?

Yes! June! Your creation, he continued to smile.

Isn't she beautiful.

I took a look at her, and almost got lost in her, Wow! I thought she was so lovely, and shined so bright.

Her red hair, the way she turned over, and over smiling as if she was lost in a fantasy, her little tiny feet, her small arms stretched out, her, just her.

8 CHAPTER

I could not get over the fact that June was in fact not my baby, I was soaking in tears, How could this be?

God, answered.

"There is not a day that goes by that one woman does not look at another woman and dare to be her, just wish to be her".

Days after the "Slumber party", Kate went behind the three of you girls and picked your Letters.

And your Letter she fell more in love with then the other two, one wanted a car, one wanted a house, we all wanted many different things, but You wanted Justin and June.

After reading your "Letter" she then too, had the eyes for Justin, but she was not so shy.

"The world is yours, but people will go behind your back and hang you with a rope".

They dated, and here today we have June.

Not physically, your, but spiritually yours, you see you envisioned her, she was literally created in your Mind, how most things are created, but there is a Strong, very strong soul-tie to creation in the Mind, he spoke, deeply.

She was everything I had ever dreamed of.

And this is very dangerous, that a world you created in your mind , has been taken over by Kate, I watch you day-dream of, "Her", June, In a big yard, with a white picket fence, while "He", Justin, watch from a distance, as he sits comfy on the porch, watching, and he smiles. I know you. Inside and out, My beautiful creation, You, Rose.

And your creation is here.

As Kate was giving birth, it was killing you, the second she pushed, was the same second you arose to death.

I walked over to Kate as she Laid there how beautifully, she looked..

I broke down, Heartbroken, How could you? My best-friend, the boy of my Dreams. Now share a Beautiful creation, my creation.

My creation.

And Justin had no idea, God added.

I cried more, more, on the hospital floor.

But, all along Rose, Yes! I designed You, and him, for you. My two lovely creations.

He was placed here, to be your Husband, The twinkle in your eyes when you laid eyes on him, allowed you to know.

A woman always knows, "My Husband" is truly written on his back, she sees it as he walks away and she smirks, he said.

Him, THE MAN, can sometimes be so blinded to her, "his Wife". He will soon turn around and see her walking away.

9 CHAPTER

Ding! Ding! Ding! Ding!

I heard in my ear, a zillion times, I rolled over and it was my alarm clock going off.

I jumped up.

OMG! I am going to be late for school, 6:30 A.M it read, and my bus came around the block at 7:00 A.M.

I rushed to shower and brushed my teeth, unwrapped my hair, and got dressed.

Grabbed my book bag. But as I picked up my bookbag a white envelope, with a red stamp on the back fell on the floor, maybe my Mother had placed it there as I was sleeping, She was now off to work.

I had no time to read it then, I ran out just in time to catch the School Bus.

As I took a seat I opened the envelope.

"You're invited to Kate Birthday Party/ Sleepover".

It read.

This was all a dream.

"There is always, and always will be a test before the gift is granted."

The end.

ABOUT THE AUTHOR

Author, Alonzeonia Rashay Ellison, Is A young black lady. Twenty-One years of age, A very beautiful soul, here to send peace,.